"I Wonder Why"

Compiled by Anna Pansini
Illustrated by Renzo Barto

Troll Associates

Library of Congress Cataloging-in-Publication Data

Pansini, Anna.
   I wonder why: questions and answers / compiled by Anna Pansini;
illustrator, Renzo Barto.
      p.   cm.—(A Question and answer book)
   Summary: First and second graders answer from their perspective a
variety of questions such as why cowboys ride horses, why
grandmothers have wrinkles, and why children have to go to school.
   ISBN 0-8167-2304-4 (lib. bdg.)   ISBN 0-8167-2305-2 (pbk.)
   1. Children's questions and answers. [1. Questions and answers.]
I. Barto, Renzo, ill. II. Title. III. Series: Question & answer
book.
AG195.P37 1991
031.02—dc20   90-44455

If you are like most kids, you wonder about many things. You have plenty of questions, and you want answers to them—fast. So we challenged kids all across America to come up with the answers to the questions they wonder about most. The response was tremendous!

The very best questions and answers were compiled and put into this book, and two others—*Kids' Question & Answer Book* and *Great Answer Book*. Each is filled with over 100 questions and answers on topics that kids are curious about.

Each contestant's name appears under the answers. Each book contains an alphabetical listing of winners, along with age or grade, school, and school address.

Finally, we'd like to thank all the students who entered the contest and the teachers who encouraged them.

I wonder why the sun shines...

The sun shines so we can see when we read, write and play. The sun shines so the plants can grow to give us food. The sun gives us energy and heat to keep us warm. The sun makes me hot when I play in the summer. The sun gives us daylight.

Holly Cron

I wonder why the sun always follows me wherever I go...

When I take a walk with my mother, the sun walks with us. When I run and look up, the sun runs with me. When I am in my father's car, the sun follows us. No matter how far he drives, the sun follows us. My mother said the sun doesn't really follow me. It just looks like it does because the sun is so big and so far away that wherever I go, I can see the sun.

Jennifer Ann Harrison

4

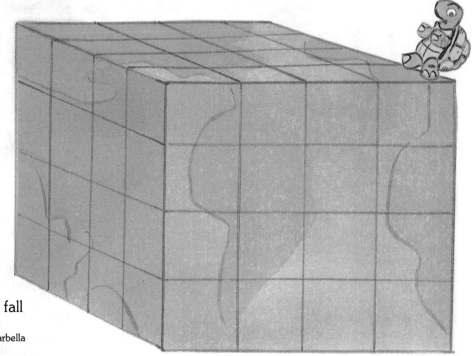

I wonder why the world is round and not square...

If the world were square, people would fall off the edge.

Jacquelyn Barbella

I wonder how stars form...

Stars form from a cloud of gas. The cloud forms a ball, which becomes a star.

Jody Mancuso

I wonder why you can't see the wind...

Wind is air that moves. Air is made of oxygen and other gases. These gases are invisible.

Brian Melancon

5

I wonder why apples fall off trees...

Because they are ripe.

Stefanie Wylie

I wonder how long plants have been on Earth...

Some people think plants have been on Earth for more than 3 billion years. The first plants were so tiny that you could see them only under a microscope. Some plants are as tall as three hundred feet. The tallest plant is the giant redwood tree. Plants come in many different shapes. Plants are neat.

Mark McDonnell

I wonder why leaves change color in the fall...

In the summer and spring, leaves are green and healthy. When fall comes, the trees know they must start storing their energy. The leaves turn colors and fall off of the trees so the tree can save its energy and make new green leaves in the spring.

Ashley Dell'Olio

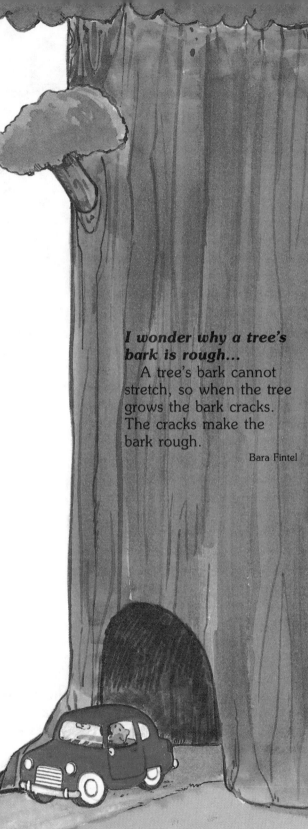

I wonder why a tree's bark is rough...

A tree's bark cannot stretch, so when the tree grows the bark cracks. The cracks make the bark rough.

Bara Fintel

I wonder why people travel to outer space...

People want to learn more about space. They want to learn about the stars and the planets. They are curious about space since no one is sure how the solar system started.

The people who travel to outer space from the United States are called astronauts. Space travelers from the Soviet Union are called cosmonauts. A Russian cosmonaut was the first man to circle the Earth in a spaceship on April 12, 1961.

There are many uses for outer space. Weather satellites are put into space to take pictures of weather patterns.

These are a few reasons why people go to outer space. The first people to land on the moon, on July 20, 1969, were U.S. astronauts. I am proud of my country, the U.S.A.

Bradley Scott Ivy

MOON
LANDING
JULY 20, 1969

SUN

MOON

EARTH

I wonder why the moon shines only at night...

The moon has no light of its own. The moon gets its light from the sun. In the daytime, the sun shines on the back of the moon. We can't see it. In the nighttime, the sun shines on the front side of the moon. That is when we see the moon shine.

Heather Caylor

I wonder why rubbing your hands together makes them warm...

Your body is made up of molecules. The molecules hold onto each other very tightly, but they are always moving—jiggling and spinning around. The molecules have energy. When you rub your hands together, you create friction. You make the molecules in your skin bump and push each other. That makes the molecules speed up. It gives them more energy. You feel the energy as heat. The faster the molecules move, the warmer you get. So if you rub your hands together hard enough they won't feel chilly any more.

Tyler Rhuems

I wonder why we have eyelashes...
To keep dust out of our eyes.

Mary Gallagher

I wonder why we need to put a cast on a broken arm or leg...

A cast will hold the bone in place while it is healing.

Grace Dyer

I wonder why people die...

Some people have a heart attack. Some people die of old age. If people didn't die, the world would be too crowded.

Jarrell Perrin

I wonder why some people wear glasses...

Because they can't see very well without glasses.

Courtney Pierce

I wonder why it doesn't hurt when I get my hair cut...

It doesn't hurt because hair does not have any nerves. Nerves carry messages of pain to our brain. When my hair gets cut there are no nerves to carry a message of pain to my brain.

Reagan Hastings

I wonder why your foot goes to sleep...

Your foot goes to sleep sometimes because the circulation of blood to your foot has been stopped. This can happen when you cross your legs or ankles for a long time or tie your shoelaces too tightly. When your foot is asleep, it feels numb and tingly and you cannot walk on it.

Haley Roberts

I wonder why I don't sink in water...

Because I am a good swimmer.

Michael Smith

I wonder why people become doctors...

They become doctors because they want to give medical treatment and help people and show love. They are good people.

Nina Bakhtiarian

I wonder why my sister does not let me touch her stuff...

Because she's afraid I might break it.

Adam Ridger

I wonder why mom and dad dance together...

Because they love each other.

Chelsey Tiller

I wonder why my sister Jennifer sucks her thumb and holds her blanket...

Jennifer does this because it makes her happy and comfortable.

Nicole Errico

I wonder why we have parents...

Because they take care of us and love us. They wipe away tears from our eyes, hug us, and make us feel better.

Deanna Boyd

I wonder why everybody likes me...

My friends like me and my family likes me. Everybody likes me. It is because I do a lot of things. I share my toys and I let people borrow things. I try to be nice to people. I even help them clean up their messes. When someone is sad, I try to cheer them up.

Zachary Medeiros

I wonder why I need a baby sitter...

I have a baby sitter when my parents go to work or out somewhere. A baby sitter keeps me out of trouble and keeps me from getting hurt.

Melanie Faust

I wonder why cowboys have horses...

They need horses so they can get to places faster.

Arick Williams

I wonder why we have holidays...

We have set aside some days as holidays for rest or play to help remember something important that happened or to honor some great person.

Meghan Leary

I wonder why boys give girls valentines...

Because they love them. Jessica Ludwig

I wonder why we celebrate Thanksgiving...

Each November people in the United States give thanks with feasting and prayer for the blessings they have received during the year. This started in 1621 with the Pilgrims of Plymouth Colony. Many other countries also have harvest celebrations. Canadians also celebrate Thanksgiving, but their Thanksgiving is celebrated in October.

Sokun Sok

I wonder why we celebrate Valentine's Day...

Because people want to show how much they care about one another. People send candy, flowers, balloons, and kisses. Friends send cards to friends to let them know how special they are. Kids give their parents cards, hugs and kisses. Valentine's Day should be every day of the year.

John Hwang

I wonder why we have birthdays...

If we didn't have birthdays, we would be zero for the rest of our lives.

Amanda Correnti

I wonder why Santa Claus wears a suit of red...

Maybe it's Mrs. Claus's favorite color, so she sewed Santa's suit with red cloth. Or maybe it's so the reindeer can easily see Santa against the white snow and can pull the sleigh right up to him. Maybe it's to match Santa's red nose and cheeks. Or maybe it's because it's a bright color and it attracts attention.

Second Graders, Haaheo School

I wonder why Santa Claus can fly with his sleigh and reindeer...

Santa can fly because the elves feed magical food to the reindeer.

Frank Alan Vocasek

I wonder what Santa Claus does in the summer...

Maybe he goes to the beach, or maybe he makes toys so that he will have enough toys for kids. Maybe he writes letters or calls kids to see if they are being good. Maybe he puts price tags on the toys so it looks like they came from a toy store. Maybe the toy stores deliver toys to him in the summer so he can give them out to the kids at Christmas.

Mike Cook

**I wonder why children
have to go to school...**

I think children should go
to school because they have
to learn in case they want to
be teachers when they grow
up.

Laura Papile

I wonder why the grass is green...

So you can tell when there is snow on the
ground. If grass were white, you wouldn't
know when it had snowed.

Daniel Webb

**I wonder why my grandmother
has wrinkles...**

I think it's because she was smiling for a
long time.

Lisa Alexander

I wonder why the stars go away
in the daytime...

    Stars stay where they are, and shine all the time. They still shine in the daytime, but we can't see them because the sunlight is too bright.

Trent McMasters

I wonder why the tooth fairy leaves two dollars...

    Because that's all she has.

Michael Kirschner

I wonder how snakes can move without legs...

Snakes can move by wriggling their bodies, gripping the ground with their bodies, pushing themselves sideways, or pressing their bellies against rocks, branches or the ground to push themselves along.

Justin Storer

I wonder why some desert animals stay underground during the day...

Some desert animals stay underground during the day to get water and stay cool because it is so hot outside in the desert.

Erin Kokomoor

I wonder why turtles have shells...

Most kinds of turtles can pull their head, legs, and tail into their shell for protection.

Jacob Reuter

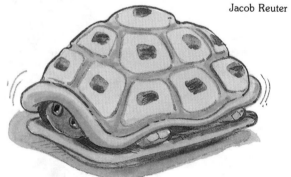

16

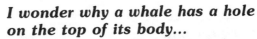

I wonder why a whale has a hole
on the top of its body...
 A whale needs the hole to help it
breathe.

Alyson Sujkowski

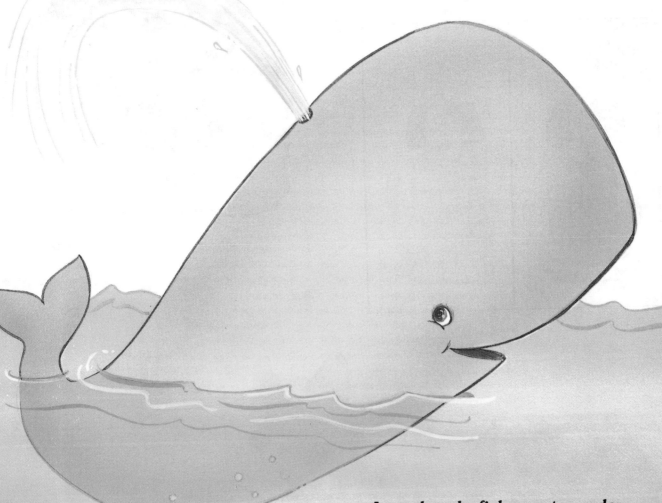

I wonder why fish can stay under
water without breathing...
 Fish do breathe, but not like humans do.
They use gills for breathing the oxygen that
is in the water. The gills are little openings
on both sides of the head. Fish take water
in through their mouths and push it out
through the gills to get oxygen.

Beth Murphree

I wonder why my dogs have so much hair in the winter and so little in the summer...

To keep warm in winter and cool in summer.

Robert Mason

I wonder why cats lick themselves all the time...

Cats lick themselves because they like to stay clean.

Katie Peters

I wonder why my dog got so big...

I think she was made to grow like that.

Alexis Kunsak

I wonder why some rabbits have floppy ears...

Because they do not have as many muscles in their ears as rabbits with straight ears. These rabbits are called lop-eared rabbits.

Craig Dershem

I wonder why my hermit crab died...
Because my brother didn't feed him.

Michael Selementi

I wonder why my parents will not let me have a horse...

Horses can be dangerous. They can strike with their hooves and fight with their teeth. Also, there are certain rules you must learn to make the horse follow your orders. You must always move and speak quietly when riding or working around a horse. A horse might even run away. And remember, don't ever walk too close behind a horse.

Eric Kasper

I wonder why bees like flowers...

Flowers are filled with a sweet liquid called nectar. Bees sip the flowers' juice and carry it to the hive in their special honey stomach. They store the nectar in cells where it ripens into thick, sweet honey.

Tonia Sirois

I wonder why mosquito bites itch...

Only female mosquitoes bite. The female mosquito sticks a long skinny part of her mouth into your skin and sucks some of your blood for food. She has a liquid in her mouth that helps her suck it up. Some of this liquid gets under your skin. A mosquito bite will itch only if you are allergic to the liquid. Most people are allergic to it, but there are a few lucky people who never get itchy mosquito bites.

Elizabeth D'Anna

20

I wonder why a jumping bean jumps...

The worm-like larva of a moth is inside the bean. The bean is really a seed. The bean jumps when the larva inside it moves.

Elias Mendoza

I wonder why termites eat wood...

Termites eat wood for food. They also build their homes in wood. The holes termites chew in the wood are their rooms. The chewed-up wood they line the rooms with is like clay.

Ricky Light

21

I wonder what the Gold Rush was...

People found gold in California in 1848. Many people began to move to California in search of gold. As years passed, more people came to California for the Gold Rush. They wanted to become rich.

Jason Paul Guana

I wonder why we have a president...

To keep and make laws for us.

Molly Harris

I wonder how Columbus discovered America...

Columbus discovered America accidentally. He was trying to find a shorter way to Asia. Instead he found America, but he thought it was Asia. He thought he was in India, and called the people in America "Indians." His ship landed at a little island Columbus named San Salvador. He sailed on the ship the *Santa Maria*.

Jose Barrios

I wonder why birds fly...

Birds fly to get places. The shape of a bird's wings helps it to fly. The bones of a bird are hollow and that helps it fly because that makes it very light. The tail is also a big help in flying. Not all birds fly. They all have two wings and two feet. Some birds fly south in cold weather. They fly south because it is too cold in the north. When the weather warms up, they fly back north.

Jaclyn Buono

I wonder how birds that fly south know when to come back...

Birds fly south because they need to find food and warmer weather. They stay until February or March. Then as the days get longer and the weather gets warmer, the birds will start flying north and return to their homes by spring. Robins are among the first birds we will see.

Tyler Callahan

I wonder why woodpeckers peck...

Woodpeckers peck because they are trying to get into the bark and wood of trees to build their nests and to get insects to eat.

Nova Morton

I wonder why the dinosaurs died out...

Scientists are not really sure why all the dinosaurs died. Some scientists think that something hit the earth very hard, making clouds of dust cover the earth. The dust blocked the sun. Without the sunlight, plants couldn't grow, the plant-eaters couldn't exist, and the meat-eating dinosaurs couldn't exist either without the plant-eaters to eat.

Maybe the temperature dropped and the dinosaurs couldn't live in the cold weather.

Maybe small egg-eating mammals ate all of the dinosaur eggs and they died out.

The seas and rivers could have dried up.

Someday I want to be a scientist, and maybe I will find the answer.

Douglas Roberts

I wonder why we sometimes can't see the moon...
Because it's on vacation.

Emily Knopf

I wonder why you have to be quiet in the library...
So other people can read their books.

Kami Swierkos

I wonder why our teachers won't let us look at other people's papers when we are taking a test...
Because our teachers want to know how much we know, not how much someone else knows.

Michael Aphibal

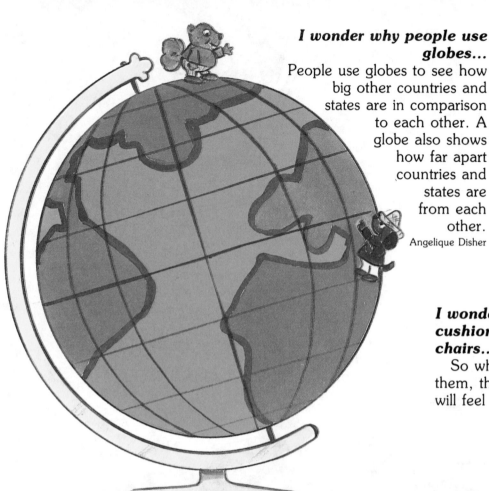

I wonder why people use globes...

People use globes to see how big other countries and states are in comparison to each other. A globe also shows how far apart countries and states are from each other.

Angelique Disher

I wonder why people put cushions in couches and chairs...

So when people sit down on them, they won't feel hard. They will feel soft.

Lance Vaillancourt

I wonder what leather is made out of...

Leather is made from an animal's skin that has been cleaned and tanned.

Meg Andrews

I wonder how milk helps make your teeth strong and healthy...

The calcium and vitamins in milk go straight to your stomach. There, they are digested and go into your blood system, which carries the calcium and vitamins to your teeth.

Julia Sutcliffe

I wonder why we have restaurants...

Because people need stuff to eat and sometimes they don't have stuff at home. We have restaurants so we will have stuff to eat and so we can eat what we like—green beans, chicken, corn, peas, and jello. You can get macaroni and cheese there and they have music and waitresses and dessert foods you can eat. You can go to a restaurant early in the morning to eat breakfast if you are going away somewhere. When you go on vacation, you can go to a restaurant to get something to eat. When you are away from home and it's time for breakfast, lunch, or dinner, you can stop at a restaurant and get something to eat instead of going all the way back to your house to get something to eat. Your waitress will give you your menu. Then you can order whatever you want to eat.

Kelly Cheek

I wonder why we pay bills...

You have to pay bills for your house so you can live in your house.

Nicholas Frame

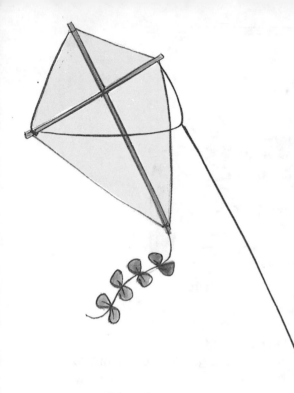

I wonder how kites fly and stay up in the air...

The wind picks up the kite and keeps it in the air. The string keeps it from flying away.

Sam Kendall

I wonder what keeps me from falling off my two-wheeled bicycle since it can't stand up by itself...

It must be my good balance.

Zachary Kumer

28

I wonder why some balloons "rise" in the air and others fall to the ground...

The balloons that rise are filled with a gas called helium that makes the balloon lighter than the air. The balloons we blow up are filled with the carbon dioxide we breathe out, which is not lighter than air so they fall unless the wind is strong and pulls them up on an air current.

Allison Pugh

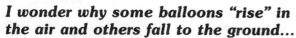

I wonder how railroad companies make tunnels in rocks and mountains...

The railroad companies use dynamite to blast the holes through hills and mountains. After the holes are blasted, dirt and rocks are carried away and pick axes are used to smooth out the tunnel.

Stephan Gambill

I wonder why the stars in the sky twinkle and shine...

Somebody puts light bulbs in them.
It's probably Santa Claus or some of the astronauts.

Ashlee Bryan

When people let go of their yellow balloons, they float up into the sky and turn into stars.

Jennifer Broyles

I think stars are really yellow light bulbs. When they break or burn out, Santa puts new yellow bulbs in them so they'll shine again.

Ernie Hicks

They twinkle because they're made of salt that somebody sprinkles around.

Brittany Neal

I wonder what shooting stars really are...

I think shooting stars are really big, white zucchinis flying high in the sky.

Bennett Coulopoulos

FLYING ZUCCHINIS

I wonder why Mars is red...
Probably because the Martians that live there have special powers to turn it red.

Jessica Deutsch

I wonder why clouds are white and fluffy...
Because they're made out of chicken feathers.

Bryan Eitelman

I wonder why the rain falls down from the sky...
God has a hundred buckets of water and he pours it down. He knows when it's time to pour the water down because he wears a watch.

Mindy Watson

I wonder why butterflies are so many different colors...

Maybe somebody painted them, or maybe they flew through a rainbow.

Joe Binkley

I wonder why chickens walk so slowly...

Because they have little feet.

Calvin Clemans

I wonder why bugs are small...

Because they don't want people to see them.

Robert Barrett

I wonder why we grow...

I think we grow so we can reach high things.

Casey Shaffer

I wonder why people grow...

I think it is so they will be big enough to get food out of the cupboard.

Carolyn Kamber

I wonder why it hurts me more now when I fall than it did when I was little...

I guess I was used to falling down a lot then.

Jeff Schulmeister

I wonder why some fish are orange...
To make the ocean colorful.

Ryan Kaney

I wonder why we have 10 fingers...
So we will have a place to wear rings.

Andrea Kern

I wonder why we have arms...
So we can give big bear hugs.

Berry Mauk

I wonder why we have fingernails...
To help us scratch when we have an itch.

Gwen Newkirk

I wonder why people have bones...
To keep them from flip-flopping.

Crystal Bowles

I wonder why people can wiggle...
I think it's because our bones are loose.

Jennifer Taylor

35

I wonder why my brother yells at the TV screen when he is playing a video game...

My brother yells at the TV screen because the game is very exciting and he wants to win.

Katie Murphy

I wonder why my mom cooks food for me...

Because I don't know how to cook.

Jackie Salisbury

I wonder why we have to go to school...

Because it's the only way to get kids out of the house every day.

Tyril Fuller

I wonder why babies cry at night...

Because they don't want to go to bed. They want to stay up and watch TV.

Candace Haynie

I wonder why my nose is on the front of my head instead of on the back of my head...

Because if I had a nose in the back of my head I would squish it every time I laid down to go to sleep. I'm glad my nose is on the front of my head.

Matt Carriger

I wonder why I don't like my little sister...

My little sister can't do anything. But she does pull my hair. She is almost 2 years old. She likes playing with her teddy bears, but she doesn't like playing with me. I wish she would let me play with her. She only has 4 teeth. Sometimes she bites me and I scream at her. Then she hits me and I run to tell Mama. I'll be glad when she gets bigger and she wants to play with me.

Kimberly Ducatte

I wonder how you cook a turkey...

I wonder how you cook a turkey...

Get a turkey at the store where they sell groceries. It will be gray, weigh about 100 pounds, feel real soft and be dead. It will have 2 legs, 1 head, 1 chest, 1 tail that used to have feathers that made a circle, and 2 feet with fingernails. It will be in a white sack. Put a little bit of grease in a pan. Wash the turkey for a minute, then put a little bit of milk on the turkey. Now put it on the pan and cook it on the stove for a little bit until it is done. Be careful and don't let the grease pop on you. You can eat bacon with this. Drink water.

Kirtis McLeskey

I wonder how you cook a turkey...

Get a turkey that looks like a chicken, but it will have its legs in back of it at the store. It will feel like soft skin but it will feel smeary too. It will cost about $29.00. You will have to wash it out with soap and a scrubber for 28 minutes. It will be raw. Find a big pan and put the turkey in it. Put not much pepper and not much salt on the turkey, then put some silver wrap over it. Then put it in the oven for 28 or 29 hours. Be sure to check on it, because when it gets done it will look like something that has not been cooked. If it looks good enough just let it cool. It will be ready to eat when it is just a little hot. Eat some potatoes, dumplings, and eggs with the turkey. Eat chocolate chip cookies and brownies for dessert. You might want some regular chicken to go with this.

DaRae Howe

I wonder how you cook a turkey...

INGREDIENTS: A 3 pound turkey; 1 teaspoon of salt; 2 squirts of watermelon juice; 3 healthy vitamins

DIRECTIONS: Take the plastic off of the turkey. Put the turkey in a saucepan. Put it into the oven for about half an hour at 10°. Take it out of the oven when one half hour has passed and cut it up. Take out the bones because we don't want to eat them. Shake on the salt. Squeeze the watermelon juice on the turkey. Put the healthy vitamins inside the turkey and eat it.

George Rakkar

Get a turkey down there at town. It will weigh 14 pounds and cost $2.00. It will be white and pink inside. It will feel froze hard. It will be in a yellow paper screen. It will have skin, meat, bones, legs, elbows, and a belly. When you get home you will have to thaw it out by boiling it in a big, big pan for 1 hour. Then put it in a big brown circle pan with a bunch of flour, 1 drip of butter, a bunch of salt and a bunch of pepper. Put it in the oven for a bunch of minutes. You will have to check it all the time to see if it is done. It will turn brown when it is done. Then you can eat some corn, potatoes, eggs, biscuits, white beans, dressing, celery, pickles, cornbread, macaroni and spaghetti. Also eat some chocolate chip cookies and drink tea, soda or water.

Virgil Condray

Get a turkey at a store. It will have 2 legs, 2 wings, a head, a nose, a mouth, a tongue, and 1 tail. It will be black and white and it will feel soft. It will be dead. When you get home you will have to soak the turkey in a sink full of vinegar for 2 hours. Then cook it on the barbecue grill for 3 hours. Then it's ready to eat with potatoes and corn. You can also make a turkey sandwich with this. Chocolate ice cream is a good dessert. Drink orange juice.

Amber Cooper

INGREDIENTS: A one pound turkey; 1 cup of salt; 2 cups of pepper.
DIRECTIONS: First you have to cut up the turkey. Then you give the turkey a shot to kill it. Put it in a big pan and cook it in the oven at 500° for about 4 minutes. Put it in the icebox and wait until it's time to eat before you take it out, but you can taste it if you want to.

D.J. Seager

INGREDIENTS: A 100 pound turkey; 2 inches of butter; 6 spoons pepper; 2 spoons salt.
DIRECTIONS: Go out to the store and look for the biggest turkey you can find. When you get it home take off the plastic. Get out all the bones and blood, and then put it in a pan. Take your hand and move the butter all over the turkey. Sprinkle on the salt and pepper and cook it for 12 hours in the oven at 500°.

Jake McDowell

Get a turkey at a store. It will weigh about 3 pounds. It will not have feathers or a head. It will be soft and it will be in a plastic bag. It will feel like a deer. It will cost $2.00. When you get home you will have to get it out of the plastic bag and put it in a square pan. Be sure to put a little toothpick in it to see if it is hot or cold. Then you will need to put 1 piece of pepper and 2 gallons of sugar on the turkey. Then just put 1 piece of bread around the turkey. Just put it in the oven for 2 hours and it will be ready to eat at 6 o'clock. You can eat mashed potatoes, corn on the cob and bread with the turkey. A good dessert is corn.

Adam Oglesby

I wonder how you cook a turkey...

Get a turkey—I don't know where. It will weigh about 40 pounds. It will have fat round legs. It will have white skin and feel like plastic. It will cost 8¢. When you get home make sure your sink is clean, then run water over the turkey for 2 minutes. If it is still dirty, run water over it for 3 more minutes. Just make sure it is not dirty before you eat that thing. Now put it on a big rectangle pan with a little bit of butter. If you like salt, put about 1 cupful on that thing. Now you cook it all through the night and through the day, but check it every two minutes. Be sure it is good and ready. You can eat peanut butter crackers with this. A good dessert is bananas. Drink sodas.

Levi Hendrix

I wonder why reading is important in our lives...

Reading is important because it is the key to learning. Being able to read makes life a great adventure.

Miriam Marie Garza

42

I wonder why we go to school...
To learn math and spelling and friendship and sharing.

Desiree Laroche

I wonder why my sister Jennifer can go to the second grade and I can't...
Because she is 7 years old and I am only 5.

Joseph Chiaramida

43

I wonder why lions have fur on their neck...

The hair around a male lion's neck makes him look bigger and stronger. It also protects him during fights. The long, thick hair softens the blows of his enemies.

Beth Crandall

I wonder why the male lion is called "the king of the jungle"...

The male lion is called "the king of the jungle" because he roars and scares the other animals. When the lion roars, he is telling the other animals that the land is his. Lions live with their families and the females hunt for food. I like lions.

Thomas Loggins

I wonder why giraffes have such long necks...

Giraffes can reach the leaves high up in trees and eat them.

Jeffrey Kaufman

I wonder why elephants have floppy ears...

Elephants use their big, floppy ears to signal other elephants. They also move them back and forth to fan themselves and cool off.

Brandon Vanderford

I wonder why an elephant has a trunk...

An elephant's nose is called a trunk. It is bigger than any other animal's nose. An elephant can feed and shower itself as well as smell with its trunk. Elephants use their trunks to move and push trees. They can carry water and food in their trunks.

Jennifer George

I wonder why tigers have stripes...

Tigers have stripes to protect them from their enemies. They use them to hide and sneak up on their prey. Stripes are important for tigers to survive and they look good, too.

Andy Stout

A Special Thanks To:

Alexander, Lisa, Grade 1, P.S. 133 Queens, Bellerose, NY

Andrews, Meg, Grade 1, Stocks Elementary, Tarboro, NC

Aphibal, Michael, Grade 1, Calvary Christian School, Pasadena, CA

Bakhtiarian, Nina, Grade 1, Mission Glen Elementary, Houston, TX

Barbella, Jacquelyn, Grade 1, Florence A. Smith School, Oceanside, NY

Barrett, Robert, Grade 1, St. Anthony School, New York City, NY

Barrios, Jose, Grade 1, Richardson Elementary, Dimmitt, TX

Binkley, Joe, Grade 1, Westbrook Elementary, Brookville, OH

Bowles, Crystal, Grade 2, Cumberland Elementary, Cumberland, VA

Boyd, Deanna, Grade 1, Bronson Elementary, Bronson, FL

Broyles, Jennifer, 5, Whitesboro Elementary, Whitesboro, TX

Bryan, Ashlee, 5, Whitesboro Elementary, Whitesboro, TX

Buono, Jaclyn, Grade 1, P.S. 11, Staten Island, NY

Callahan, Tyler, Grade 1, Hoosick Falls Central School, Hoosick Falls, NY

Carriger, Matt, Grade 1, Sacred Heart School, Ottawa, KS

Caylor, Heather, Grade 1, Lambert Elementary, Manchester, IA

Cheek, Kelly, 6, John Hancock Academy, Sparta, GA

Chiaramida, Joseph, 5, Saint Helena's School, Edison, NJ

Clemans, Calvin, Grade 1, Bailly School, Chesterton, IN

Condray, Virgil, Kindergarten, Marmaduke Elementary, Lafe, AR

Cook, Mike, Grade 1, Willow Springs Elementary, Centreville, VA

Cooper, Amber, Kindergarten, Marmaduke Elementary, Lafe, AR

Correnti, Amanda, Grade 1, St. Dominic Savio School, St. Louis, MO

Coulopoulos, Bennett, Grade 1, Bailly School, Chesterton, IN

Crandall, Beth, Grade 2, Timothy Ball School, Crown Point, IN

Cron, Holly, Grade 1, Shannon Elementary, Shannon, MS

D'Anna, Elizabeth, Grade 1, P.S. 11 Richmond, Staten Island, NY

Dell'Olio, Ashley, Grade 1, P.S. 11 Richmond, Staten Island, NY

Dershem, Craig, Grade 1, Sanborn Elementary, Longmont, CO

Deutsch, Jessica, Grade 1, P.S. 133 Queens, Bellerose, NY

Disher, Angelique, Grade 1, Carroll Elementary, Southlake, TX

Ducatte, Kimberly, Grade 1, Stocks Elementary, Tarboro, NC

Dyer, Grace, Grade 1, Carroll Elementary, Southlake, TX

Eitelman, Bryan, 5, Whitesboro Elementary, Whitesboro, TX

Errico, Nicole, Grade 1, P.S. 11 Richmond, Staten Island, NY

Faust, Melanie, Grade 1, Thomas Public Schools, Thomas, OK

Fintel, Bara, Grade 1, South School, Glencoe, IL

Frame, Nicholas, Grade 1, St. Francis Xavier School, Moundsville, WV

Fuller, Tyril, Grade 2, Cumberland Elementary, Cumberland, VA

Gallagher, Mary, Grade 1, Bronson Elementary, Bronson, FL

Gambill, Stephan, 4, Margaret Ave. Child Care Center, Terre Haute, IN

Garza, Miriam Marie, 6, Cromack Elementary, Brownsville, TX

George, Jennifer, Grade 1, P.S. 11 Richmond, Staten Island, NY

Guana, Jason Paul, Grade 1, Richardson Elementary, Dimmitt, TX

Harris, Molly, Grade 1, St. Dominic Savio School, St. Louis, MO

Harrison, Jennifer Ann, Grade 1, P.S. 11 Richmond, Staten Island, NY

Hastings, Reagan, Grade 1, Central Elementary, Seaford, DE

Haynie, Candace, 5, Whitesboro Elementary, Whitesboro, TX

Hendrix, Levi, Kindergarten, Marmaduke Elementary, Lafe, AR

Hicks, Ernie, 6, Whitesboro Elementary, Whitesboro, TX

Howe, DaRae, Kindergarten, Marmaduke Elementary, Lafe, AR

Hwang, John, Grade 2, School #3, Fort Lee, NJ

Ivy, Bradley Scott, Grade 1, Shannon Elementary, Shannon, MS

Kamber, Carolyn, Grade 1, Bailly Elementary, Chesterton, IN

Kaney, Ryan, Grade 1, Thomas Public Schools, Thomas, OK

Kasper, Eric, Grade 1, Sheridan Elementary, Sheridan, TX

Kaufman, Jeffrey, Grade 1, Arcadia School, Olympia Fields, IL

Kendall, Sam, Kindergarten, Rives Elementary, Rives, TN

Kern, Andrea, 7, Lincoln School, Bedford, IN

Kirschner, Michael, Grade 1, Florence A. Smith School, Oceanside, NY

Knopf, Emily, 7, Ranney School, Tinton Falls, NJ

Kokomoor, Erin, Grade 2, Vineland Elementary, Rotunda West, FL

Kumer, Zachary, Grade 1, Edgeworth Elementary, Edgeworth, PA

Kunsak, Alexis, Grade 1, Edgeworth Elementary, Edgeworth, PA

Laroche, Desiree, Grade 1, Bronson Elementary, Bronson, FL

Leary, Meghan, Grade 2, Auburn Village School, Auburn, NH

Light, Ricky, Grade 1, P.S. 11 Richmond, Staten Island, NY

Loggins, Thomas, Grade 1, P.S. 11 Richmond, Staten Island, NY

Ludwig, Jessica, Grade 1, Taft Elementary, Lawton, OK

Mancuso, Jody, Grade 2, Spring Garden Elementary, Bedford, TX

Mason, Robert, Grade 1, Central Elementary, Seaford, DE

Mauk, Berry, Grade 1, Oakview Elementary, Ashland, KY

McDonnell, Mark, Grade 2, Spring Garden Elementary, Bedford, TX

McDowell, Jake, 5, Whitesboro Elementary, Whitesboro, TX

McLeskey, Kirtis, Kindergarten, Marmaduke Elementary, Lafe, AR

McMasters, Trent, Grade 1, Shannon Elementary, Shannon, MS

Medeiros, Zachary, Grade 1, Walley School, Bristol, RI

Melancon, Brian, Grade 1, M.E. Norman Elementary, Morgan City, LA

Mendoza, Elias, Grade 1, Canutillo Elementary, Canutillo, TX

Morton, Nova, 8, Farrington School, Augusta, ME

Murphree, Beth, Grade 1, Shannon Elementary, Shannon, MS

Murphy, Katie, Grade 1, H.A. Marsh School, Absecon, NJ

Neal, Brittany, 6, Whitesboro Elementary, Whitesboro, TX

Newkirk, Gwen, Grade 1, Rincon Elementary, Rincon, GA

Oglesby, Adam, Kindergarten, Marmaduke Elementary, Lafe, AR

Papile, Laura, Grade 1, P.S. 133 Queens, Bellerose, NY

Perrin, Jarrell, Grade 1, Mission Glen Elementary, Houston, TX

Peters, Katie, Grade 2, Mayfield Elementary, Mayfield, NY

Pierce, Courtney, Grade 1, Carroll Elementary, Southlake, TX

Pugh, Allison, 3, Margaret Ave. Child Care Center, Terre Haute, IN

Rakkar, George, 6, Whitesboro Elementary, Whitesboro, TX

Reuter, Jacob, Grade 2, Table Mound School, Dubuque, IA

Rhuems, Tyler, Grade 1, George Nettels School, Pittsburg, KS

Ridger, Adam, Grade 1, Jackling Elementary, West Valley City, UT

Roberts, Douglas, Kindergarten, Alton Elementary, Alton, MO

Roberts, Haley, Grade 1, Carroll Elementary, Southlake, TX

Salisbury, Jackie, Grade 1, Calvary Christian School, Pasadena, CA

Schulmeister, Jeff, Grade 1, Edgeworth Elementary, Edgeworth, PA

Seager, D.J., 5, Whitesboro Elementary, Whitesboro, TX

Second Graders, Haaheo School, Hilo, HI

Selementi, Michael, Grade 1, Northvail School, Parsippany, NJ

Shaffer, Casey, Grade 2, Hydetown School, Titusville, PA

Sirois, Tonia, 7, Farrington School, Augusta, ME

Smith, Michael, Kindergarten, Saint Helena's School, Edison, NJ

Sok, Sokun, 8, Garden Elementary, Venice, FL

Storer, Justin, Grade 1, Arcadia School, Olympia Fields, IL

Stout, Andy, Grade 1, Chapin Elementary, Chapin, SC

Sujkowski, Alyson, Grade 1, Ladyfield School, Toledo, OH

Sutcliffe, Julia, Kindergarten, Stanlick School, Wharton, NJ

Swierkos, Kami, Grade 1, St. Francis Xavier School, Moundsville, WV

Taylor, Jennifer, Grade 1, Edgeworth Elementary, Edgeworth, PA

Tiller, Chelsey, Grade 1, Republican Valley Elementary, Indianola, NE

Vaillancourt, Lance, Grade 1, Prairie Heights Elementary, LaGrange, IN

Vanderford, Brandon, Grade 1, Carroll Elementary, Southlake, TX

Vocasek, Frank Alan, Grade 1, P.S. 133 Queens, Bellerose, NY

Watson, Mindy, 6, Whitesboro Elementary, Whitesboro, TX

Webb, Daniel, Grade 1, Centerville Elementary, Centerville, UT

Williams, Arick, Grade 1, Taft Elementary, Lawton, OK

Wylie, Stefanie, Grade 1, Jackson Christian School, Jackson, TN